10 places to eat LONDON

"Less is More"

A guide to 10 places serving exceptional traditional food, for the business traveller and leisure traveller wanting to try something different.

By Tagore Ramoutar

www.10placestoeat.com

First Published in 2010.
Published by Longshot Ventures Ltd, UK.
Printed in the UK.
First Edition Hardback. ISDN 978-1-907837-00-5

Copyright Tagore Ramoutar, Longshot Ventures Ltd.
The rights of Tagore Ramoutar to be identified
as the author and photographer of this work has been
asserted by him in accordance with the
Copyright, Designs and Patents Act, 1988.
All rights reserved.

Introduction to
10 places to eat guides

The inspiration behind 10 places to eat was the frustration of travelling on business and being brought to very nice international or French restaurants no matter which country in the world I was in. Even where the food was nominally local it wasn't really traditional food. When I visited Japan, which I went to regularly for three years, I had the freedom to choose and I typically went to little local restaurants who served one type of food very well. Also when business visitors came to London they frequently asked for recommendations for a Pub, Fish & Chips or a Curry.

Most guide books overwhelm the reader with choice, and it is difficult to make a decision. This book is based on the premise that most visitors to a city, whether on business or leisure, rarely visit for more than a week, and therefore only need a few choices. This book collects together a very personal view of restaurant recommendations for London. It is especially relevant for those interested in exploring typical English food served in traditional settings. The recommendations have been visited and sampled by myself as a paying customer. Many of these restaurants have been visited many times and retain a firm place in my heart and memories. Some are well known, others not. All are long established and are generally not trendy and or run by well known chefs. Typically their menus don't really change from year to year, though many will have a strong seasonal influence and serve traditional dishes usually using British ingredients. Some are not typical business restaurants and are not really suitable at all for business meals (these will be highlighted).

The book and the recommendations are not meant to be comprehensive rather reflect the areas that I have spent most time and my tastes. I hope you can also enjoy them as much as I have.

Introduction to 10 places to eat LONDON

The London guide recommends 10 places to experience traditional English food. All the places selected are established businesses with a longstanding reputation and could be considered amongst the best in the genre. The focus of the guide is to give the visitor a taste of local food, it does not seek to rank the different types or select the latest in-restaurant. Places selected have both excellent food and an authentic traditional atmosphere. In many of the places the menu does not change so a recommended meal has been selected. Note prices were correct in Spring 2010.

The guide gives a history / background of the venue and type of food, a recommended menu and a walking map to get there from the nearest Underground Station.

The London Guide covers main well known traditional food dishes but also tries to cover the occasions such as Afternoon Tea that are so part of English culture.

The choice of restaurants includes London's oldest, Rules, established in 1798, plus two pubs serving food to give the visitor the pub experience. The newest restaurant recommended, Roast opened in 2005, is located in Britain's oldest known food market. For the Fish & Chip recommendation I have selected a traditional cafe. Unusually I have also recommended an Indian restaurant; whilst not strictly English, Indian food has become very much part of English culture, and many visitors to London try and fit a curry in while they are here if they get the opportunity.

10 meals to eat
10 places to eat

Oysters and Fish at Bentley's, Nr Piccadilly

Sunday Lunch (Roast Beef and Yorkshire Pudding) at Roast, Borough Market

Steak & Kidney Pie at The Guinea Grill, Mayfair

Game and Puddings at Rules, London's oldest restaurant located in Covent Garden

English Breakfast at Simpson's-in-the-Strand

Afternoon Tea at Fortnum & Mason, Piccadilly

Experience gastropub food at The Anchor & Hope in Waterloo

The Punjab for a Curry, Chicken Tikka Masala, in Covent Garden

Jellied Eels and Pie 'n' Mash at Manze, Bermondsey just south of Tower Bridge

Fish & Chips at the Golden Hind, just north of Oxford St

The locations of the recommendations
Central London - West End

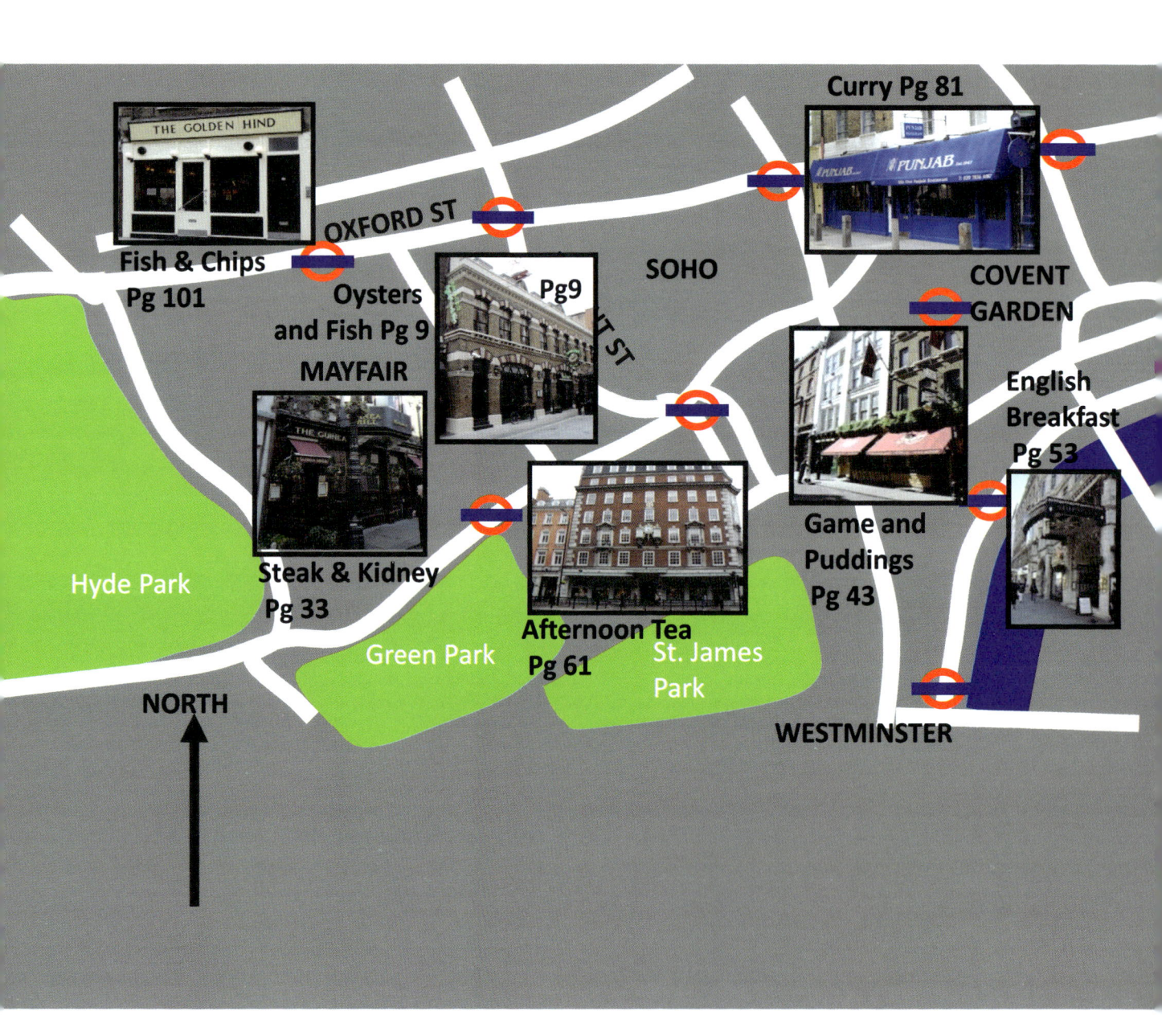

The City and South of the River

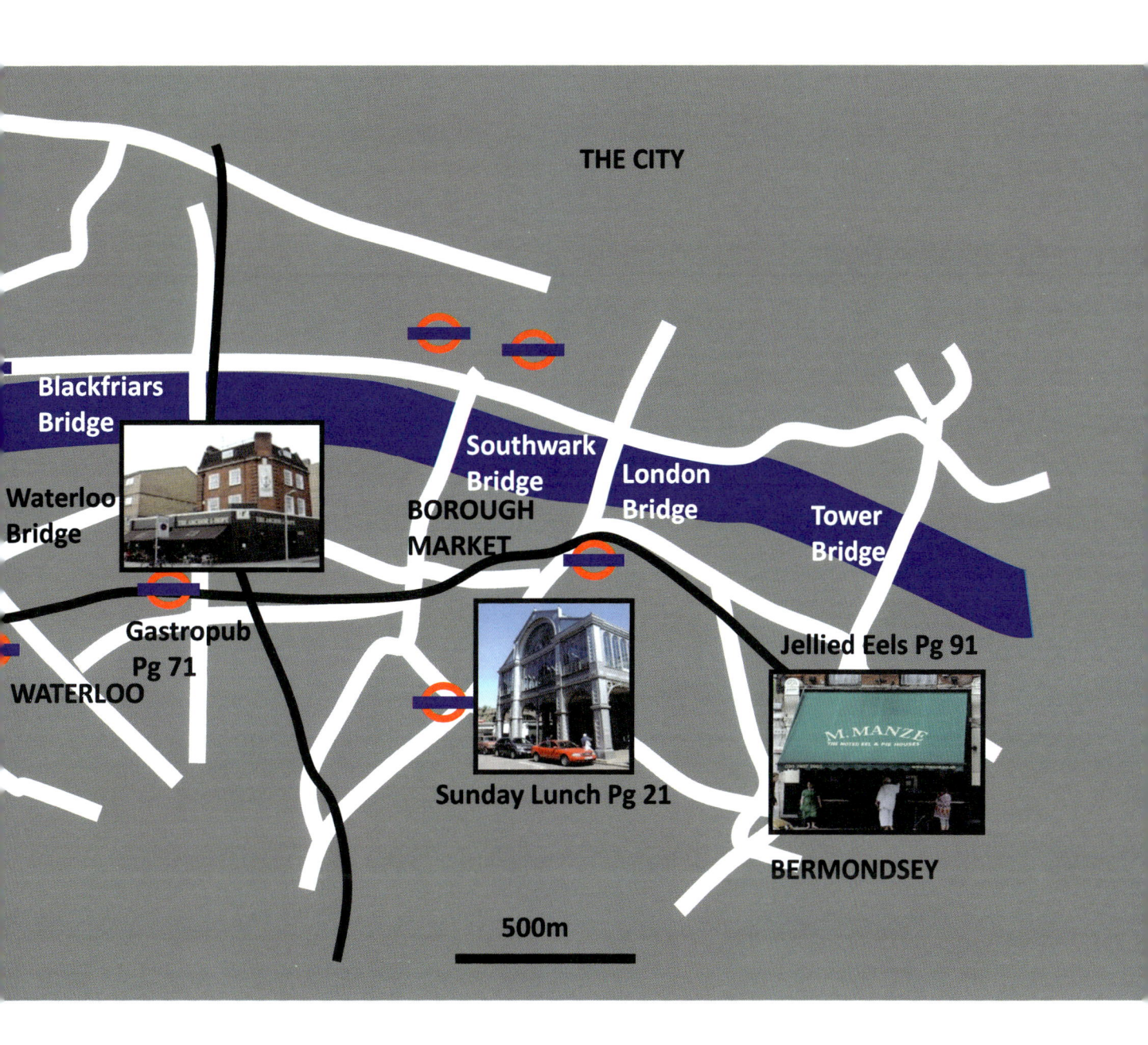

Oysters and Fish
Bentley's

Bentley's Background

Bentley's was opened as an oyster bar and grill in 1916 by the Bentley family who owned their own oyster beds in West Mersea near Colchester. The restaurant is located on Swallow Street, a short connecting street between Regent Street and Piccadilly, and is housed in a Victorian building, with an arts and crafts movement-inspired interior and an Italian-gothic façade.

Oyster rooms are a long established part of London dining and provide the opportunity for informal supper, especially for theatre goers.

From the start Bentley's was dedicated to simple quality seafood and it soon became fashionable and continued to be popular haunt for seafood lovers throughout the twenties and thirties. After the Second World War Bentley's was once again recognized as one of London's pre-eminent Fish and Oyster restaurants.

In 1948 the editor of Dining Out, wrote:

"Probably the best lobster soup in the world".

In 1956 the editor of Invitations to Dine, wrote:

"To all those interested in fish, the name of Bentley's has become a household word."

By 1961 the restaurant critic Egon Ronay, wrote:

"The two Mr Bentley's are not only excellent restaurateurs; they are also oyster farmers who sell their delicious produce all over the country."

In the 1990s Richard Corrigan arrived as head chef, and in 2005 he took over the restaurant. Now refurbished, Bentley's is still one of London's best loved Oyster Bar and Grill restaurants.

Bentley's
Swallow St, Nr Piccadilly

Bentley's Oyster Bar
Swallow St, Nr Piccadilly

Bentley's
11-15 Swallow Street, W1B 4DG
Tel +44 (0)20 7734 4756

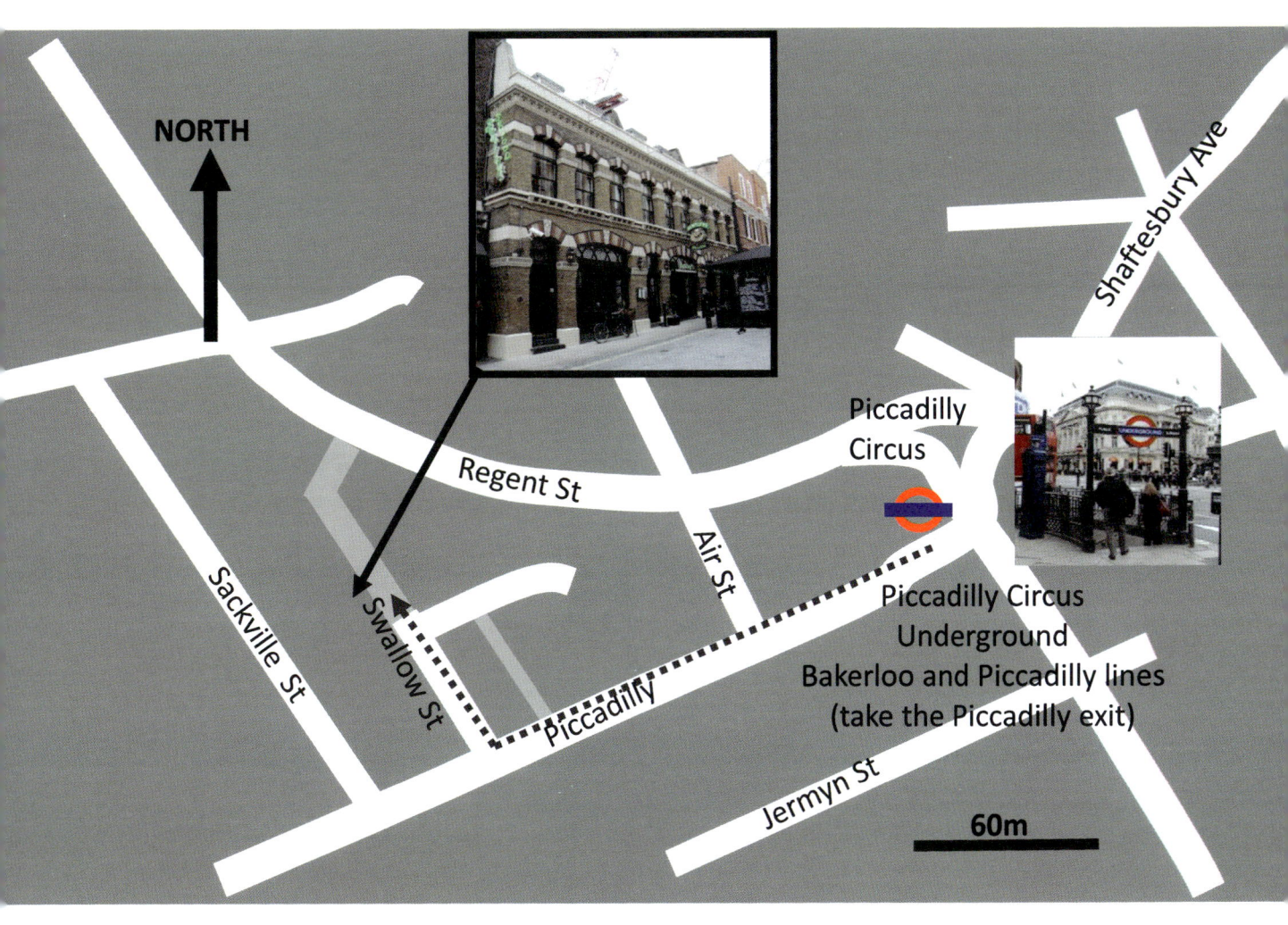

Piccadilly Circus
Piccadilly Circus Underground
Bakerloo and Piccadilly lines
(take the Piccadilly exit)

Open seven days a week (need to book):

Oyster & Champagne Bar
Monday – Saturday		12.00-24.00
Sunday		12.00-22.00

The Grill
Monday – Saturday	Lunch	12.00-15.00
	Dinner	18.00-23.00
Sunday	Dinner	18.00-22.00

www.bentleys.org

Oysters
Background

London has long been a city that loves fish and seafood, in fact in the 1800s London's pre-eminent fish market, Billingsgate Market, was the largest in the world. Many of the London's oldest restaurants still specialise in fish and have oyster bars.

Oysters have been cultivated in Britain since Roman times, and native oysters are highly prized. Nowadays oysters are thought of as a luxury and an indulgence, and to some an aphrodisiac, however in times past they were the food of the poor and were often used in Steak and Kidney pies as a substitute to fill out the pie.

Typically oysters are served raw and are presented in their half shell. Usually you order 6, 9 or 12 (a dozen) and the oysters are sucked from the shell raw or with a dressing or lemon. Note fresh oysters must be alive just before consumption (to be safe); there is a simple criterion for finding out if it is alive, a live oyster will close up when tapped on the shell.

The term Oyster Bar is used to describe a restaurant or bar specialising in serving fresh oysters, shucked behind a counter in sight of the customers. Typically, where a restaurant has an Oyster Bar and a Grill room, the Oyster Bar is more informal and has a shorter menu; oysters are generally available in both.

Nine Oysters
Bentley's

Oysters and Fish at Bentley's Recommended Menu

Bentley's is almost exclusively a fish and seafood restaurant. There are three different dinning experiences The Grill upstairs, an outside eating area and the Oyster Bar on the ground floor. The Oyster Bar is the recommended option; it has a busy informal but smart atmosphere. In the Oyster Bar there are both tables and bar seating.

Whilst this is one of the more expensive of the recommendations it makes a great evening out, especially if combined with drinks at the Champagne bar. The Oyster Bar itself is full of atmosphere and is a great place to people watch. Note it is imperative to book, and during the week sittings are strictly 2 hours only.

The recommended meal is Oysters followed by Dover Sole.

For the starter it is recommended to order nine mixed selection oysters. If raw oysters are a little too much then the smoked salmon is wonderful.

The main course chosen is Meuniere Dover sole, this is a typical dish of London and is a simple classic. Dover sole is a flat fish that has a mild, buttery sweet flavour. Note the prices are quoted based on the daily market price and weight. Order a side dish of either chips or new potatoes when in season. Again an alternative choice for main course is Fish Pie which is amongst the best in London.

For dessert try the trifle which is a modern take on an English classic.

The three course meal recommended, excluding drinks and service, costs approximately £80* per person.

*2010 prices.

Meuniere Dover Sole
Bentley's

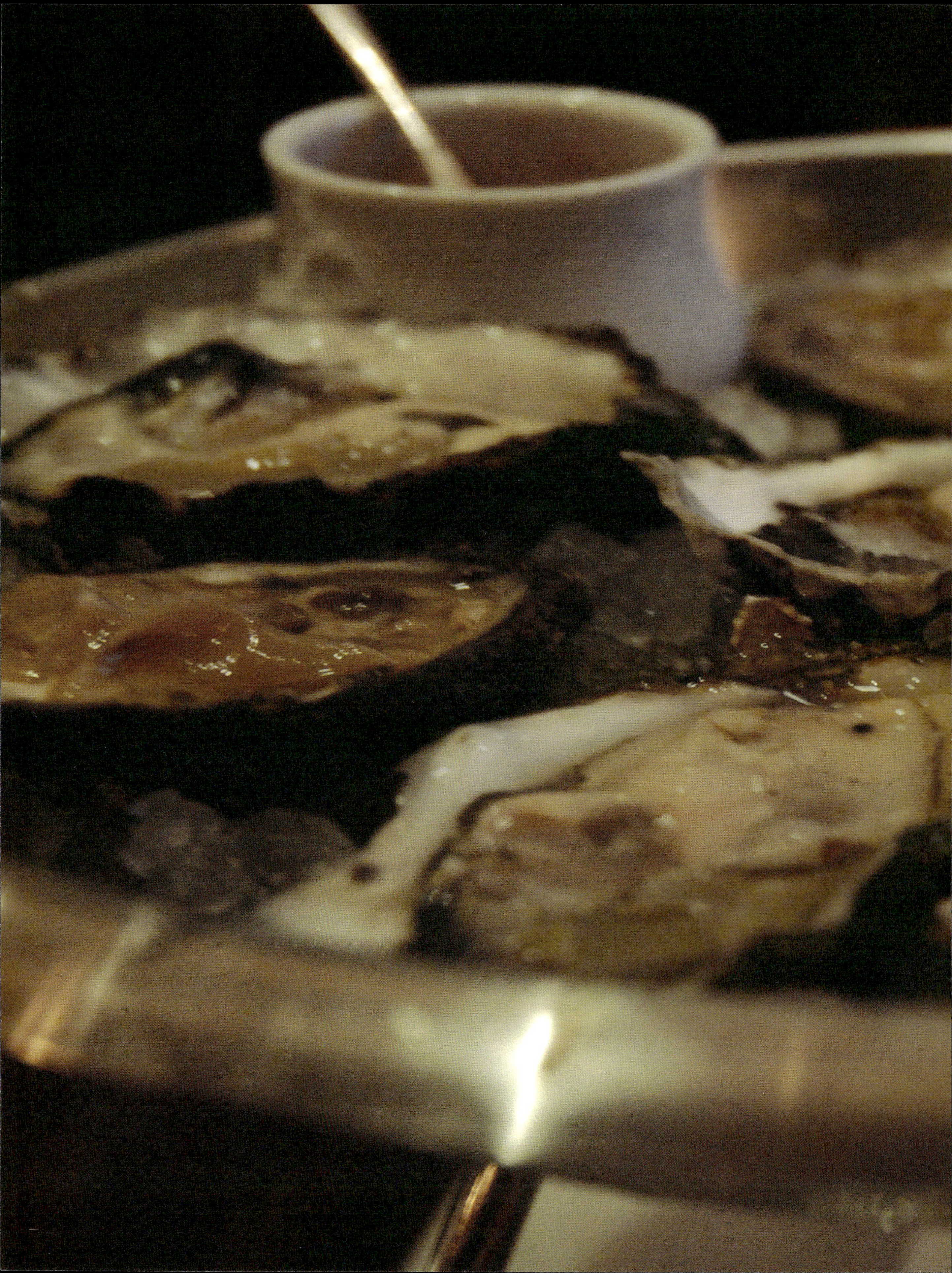

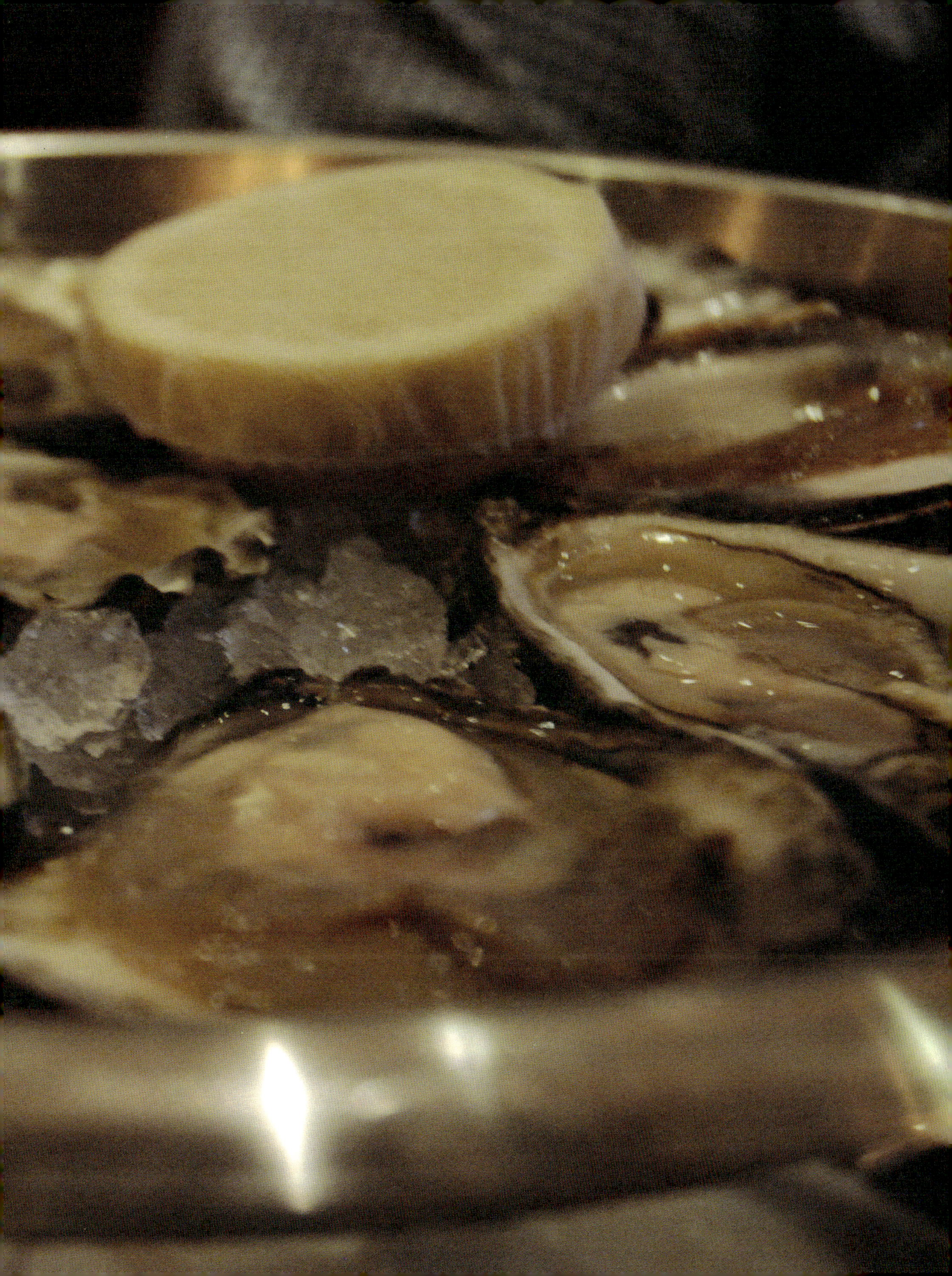

Roast Beef and Yorkshire Pudding /Sunday Lunch Roast

Roast
Background

Roast specialises in classic British cooking using seasonal products from the UK. It was set up in Borough Market in 2005 by Iqbal Wahhab, the founder of the award winning modern Indian restaurant the Cinnamon Club, and is the located above Borough Market in the beautiful portico of the former flower market.

Borough Market is one of the oldest markets in Britain dating back to Roman times, though the first formal mention is recorded in 1276.

The present market buildings date from 1851, with the art deco entrance added on Southwark Street in 1932. The market is still a functioning wholesale market as well a retail one. It now specialises in organic fruit, vegetables and rare breeds' meats – it is now essentially the gastro-market of London.

If you want to see the market you need to visit Roast on a week day or Saturday. The wholesale market is open weekday mornings (02.00-08.00) and the retail market operates only on Thursdays (11.00-17.00), Fridays (12.00-18.00), and Saturdays from (09.00-17.00).

Roast's menu is strongly seasonal and the ingredients are sourced from all over the UK. Each day there are specials, certain meals such as Roast Beef and Yorkshire Pudding are generally only available on a Sunday. Whilst roast beef is the recommended meal, it is a good place for lamb and pork and chicken also. On a Sunday, roast beef is part of a three course set meal, which costs in 2010 £30 per person excluding drinks.

Note Roast is situated on the first floor over-looking the market and you get a great view of the bustling market during the week. To get to Roast walk into the market and the entrance is in the centre.

Roast
Borough Market

Roast
Borough Market

Roast
The Floral Hall, Stoney Street, SE1 1TL
Tel +44(0)845 034 7300

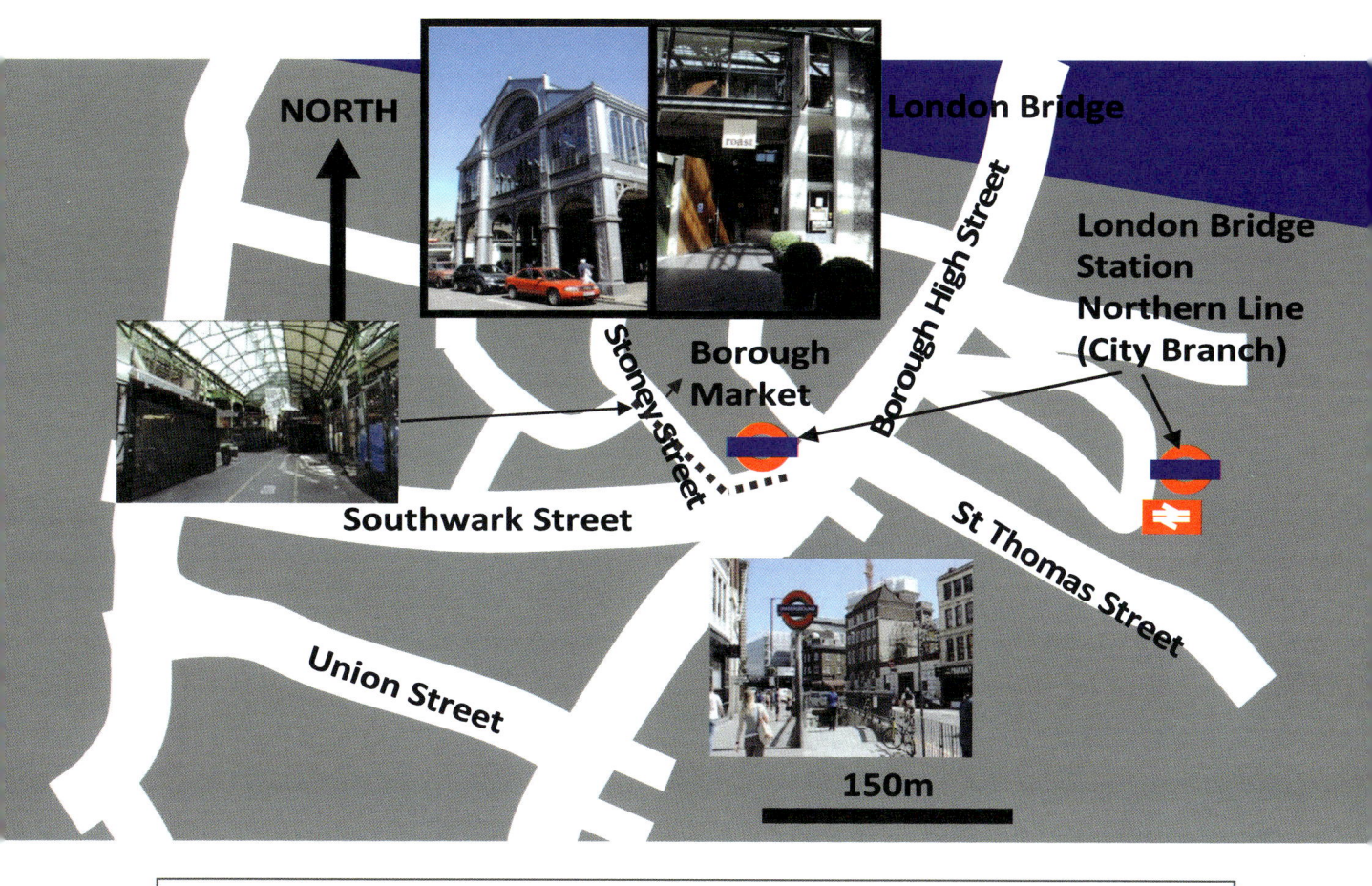

Open seven days a week (need to book):		
Breakfast:	Monday to Friday	07.00-11.00
	Saturday	08.00-11.30
Lunch:	Monday to Wednesday	12.00-14.45
	Thursday to Friday	12.00-15.45
	Saturday	12.15-15.45
	Sunday	11.30-18.00
Dinner:	Monday to Friday	17.30-22.30
	Saturday	18.00-22.30

www.roast-restaurant.com

Roast Beef and Yorkshire Pudding Background

If there is one formal meal associated with Britain it is Roast Beef and Yorkshire Pudding. It is traditionally served on a Sunday at midday and is known as Sunday Lunch. Often treated as a special occasion; Sunday Lunch, whether eaten out or at home, is essentially a family affair and is the one meal in a week that families will still try and eat together.

The tradition of Sunday Roast is thought to date back to feudal times and probably originates from the practice of the local squire rewarding his serfs for the week's work by sharing a meal of roast oxen every Sunday.

Sunday Lunch or Sunday Roast will typically be roast meat, roast potatoes and vegetables. Whilst beef is the most famous choice, chicken, lamb or pork are common and a selection is generally offered in most restaurants serving Sunday Lunch. Each meat has separate condiments / accompaniments that are only served with the particular meat i.e. beef with Yorkshire pudding and horseradish; chicken with stuffing and bread sauce; pork with crackling (crisp skin) and apple sauce; and lamb with mint sauce. All are served with gravy made from the juices of the roasted meat, roast potatoes and 1-3 types of vegetables typically boiled (carrots or cabbage) or roasted (parsnips).

Roast beef is traditionally served "rare" or "pink", meaning that the centre of the joint is warmed, but not cooked so that it retains the red colour of raw beef. The traditional accompaniment for roast beef is Yorkshire pudding, this is a light savoury batter pudding cooked in the hot fat from the roast. First recorded in 1737, the Yorkshire pudding originates from the northern county of Yorkshire but is now very much a national English dish. In Yorkshire is it often eaten separately or with a variety of meats, however in the rest of the country it is only eaten with roast beef.

Joint of Roast Beef

Sunday Lunch at Roast Recommended Menu

If you are staying over a weekend and have company it is recommended that you try a traditional Sunday Lunch. It is served in most British Restaurants and most pubs. Typically it is eaten between 12.00 and 14.00.

Usually Sunday Lunch does not come with a starter, though restaurants will all offer starters; the main course followed by a pudding should be sufficient.

Roast (the restaurant) is a great place to have Sunday Lunch. Its light, airy ambience plus relaxed service are combined with excellent food to provide a great experience. After, if the weather is nice, you can walk along the River Thames all the way from Borough Market to Westminster – you pass The Globe (a replica of Shakespeare's original theatre), past the Tate Modern and all the way to the London Eye.

Whilst the recommended meal is roast beef, it is a good place for chicken, lamb and pork also. The menu is strongly seasonal and ingredients sourced from all over the UK, therefore the accompanying vegetables will change throughout the year. Note each day there are specials and roast beef is generally only available on a Sunday. On a Sunday the roast beef is part of a 2 or 3 course set meal, costing £26/ £30* excluding drinks and service.

It is recommended that you have Roast Beef and Yorkshire Pudding followed by a traditional dessert with custard.

If you are not staying over the weekend but still want to try Roast Beef and Yorkshire Pudding, Simpson's-in-the-Strand serve it daily during the week.

*2010 prices.

Roast Beef and Yorkshire Pudding
Roast

Alternative Sunday Lunch
Roast Chicken with Bread Sauce
Roast

Apple and Raspberry Crumble with Custard Roast

Steak & Kidney Pie
The Guinea Grill

The Guinea Grill
Background

The Guinea is a traditional English pub in the heart of Mayfair, located on Bruton Place. It dates back to 1675 and was the local watering hole for the stable hands and servants employed by the rich and wealthy residents of Berkeley Square and Bruton Street.

It has been a Young's Pub since 1888 – Young's is a traditional London beer brewing company. Close to Bond Street, The Guinea still serves the people who work locally, particularly the surveyor trade.

The Guinea has a traditional pub in front and a cosy grill restaurant in the rear. The grill restaurant opened in 1953 with one small dining room and a coal fired grill. The restaurant specialises in steak, lamb, fresh fish and seafood, and famous award winning Steak & Kidney Pies.

The Guinea Grill is a great place for casual pint and pub snacks as well as more formal dinning in the back grill room. The restaurant is full of character and is now spread over two separate rooms. Note: To get to the Grill restaurant enter by the left-hand door.

The Guinea Grill
Mayfair

The Guinea Grill
Mayfair

The Guinea Grill
30 Bruton Place, Mayfair, W1J 6NL
Tel +44 (0)20 7499 1210

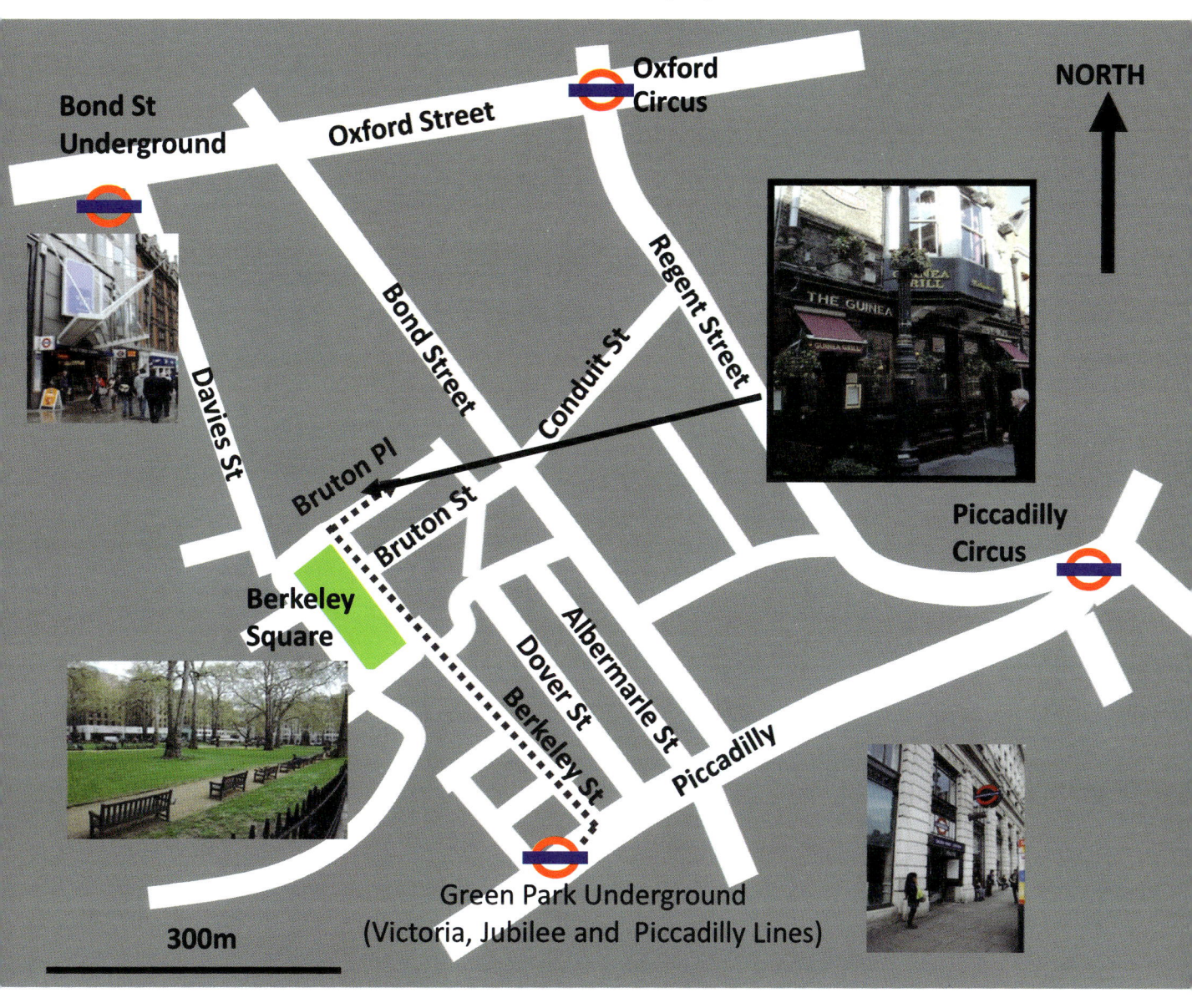

Open six days a week (need to book especially for lunch):

Monday to Friday	12:30-15:00
	18:00-22:30
Saturday	18:00-22:30

www.theguinea.co.uk

Steak & Kidney Pie
Background

Pies are quintessentially British, with Wikipedia listing 39 different main types, both savoury and sweet, running from Pork Pies to Apple Pies. A pie is defined as a baked dish of ingredients, either savoury or sweet, encased in or topped with pastry. They can be served hot or cold depending on the pie.

The pie chosen as the most traditional is the Steak and Kidney Pie. It consists of a filling of diced beef steak and kidneys in a thick sauce typically consisting of beef broth, flavoured with salt, pepper, parsley and onions. It is usually a one-crust pie i.e. filling is covered only by a pastry lid, not encased; the pastry is usually hot water crust pastry but can be puff pastry or short crust pastry.

There are variations of the dish, most commonly Steak Pie, Steak and Ale Pie, Steak and Mushroom Pie or Steak and Kidney Pudding (a steamed version using suet pastry).

Many of the restaurants in this guide serve pies, however the Guinea Grill has been chosen as it has won awards for its pies and also gives you a chance to experience a lovely local pub at the same time.

Steak & Kidney Pie
The Guinea Grill

Steak & Kidney Pie or Steak & Mushroom Pie at the Guinea Grill Recommended Meal

The Guinea Grill is very close to Bond Street so is an excellent place for a lunch or an early dinner after shopping. It is also a nice pub and serves a good pint of Young's beer. It is recommended to either start or finish with a pint in the bar.

If you are only going to the restaurant please enter via the left-hand door, the right hand door leads to the pub.

The recommended meal is Steak and Kidney Pie or Steak and Mushroom Pie with side dishes of chips, green beans and mushrooms. One set of the side dishes should be sufficient for two. The pies are large (very large) so once again two courses are generally sufficient, either a starter or main or main course with dessert.

Cost per person is approximately £25.00* for the main course and side dishes only and excluding service and drinks.

*2010 prices.

Steak & Mushroom Pie
The Guinea Grill

Game and Puddings Rules

Rules
Background

Rules is the oldest private restaurant in London, dating back to 1798, when it was originally opened as an Oyster Bar. In its long history it has only been owned by three families. Until early 20th Century it was owned by the Rule family; just before the Great War Charles Rule swapped it for a Parisian restaurant owned by Tom Bell, whose daughter sold it to the present owner John Mayhew in 1984.

Rules serves traditional seasonal English food, it specialises in classic game cookery, pies and puddings. Rules owns its own game estate, the Lartington Estate, in the Pennines. It provides high quality game birds and roe deer in season and Belted Galloway beef. The Game Season dictates the menus; to a certain extent most game birds and fowl are in Season during the second half of the year, some examples are shown below:

Red Grouse & Ptarmigan	12 Aug - 10 Dec
Partridge	1 Sept - 1 Feb
Wild Duck and Geese (Inland)	1 Sept - 31 Jan
Pheasant	1 Oct - 1 Feb
Deer Roe Buck	1 Apr - 31 Oct
Deer Roe Doe	1 Nov - 28/29 Feb

The atmosphere is very old English, you are even greeted by a doorman in a top hat. Though slightly touristy, it is still heavily used by business people and parents of students. The clientele is slightly older than average and the restaurant is suitable for business guests and for very long lunches.

Rules
Covent Garden

Rules
Covent Garden

Rules
35 Maiden Lane, Covent Garden, WC2E 7LB
Tel +44 (0)20 7836 5314

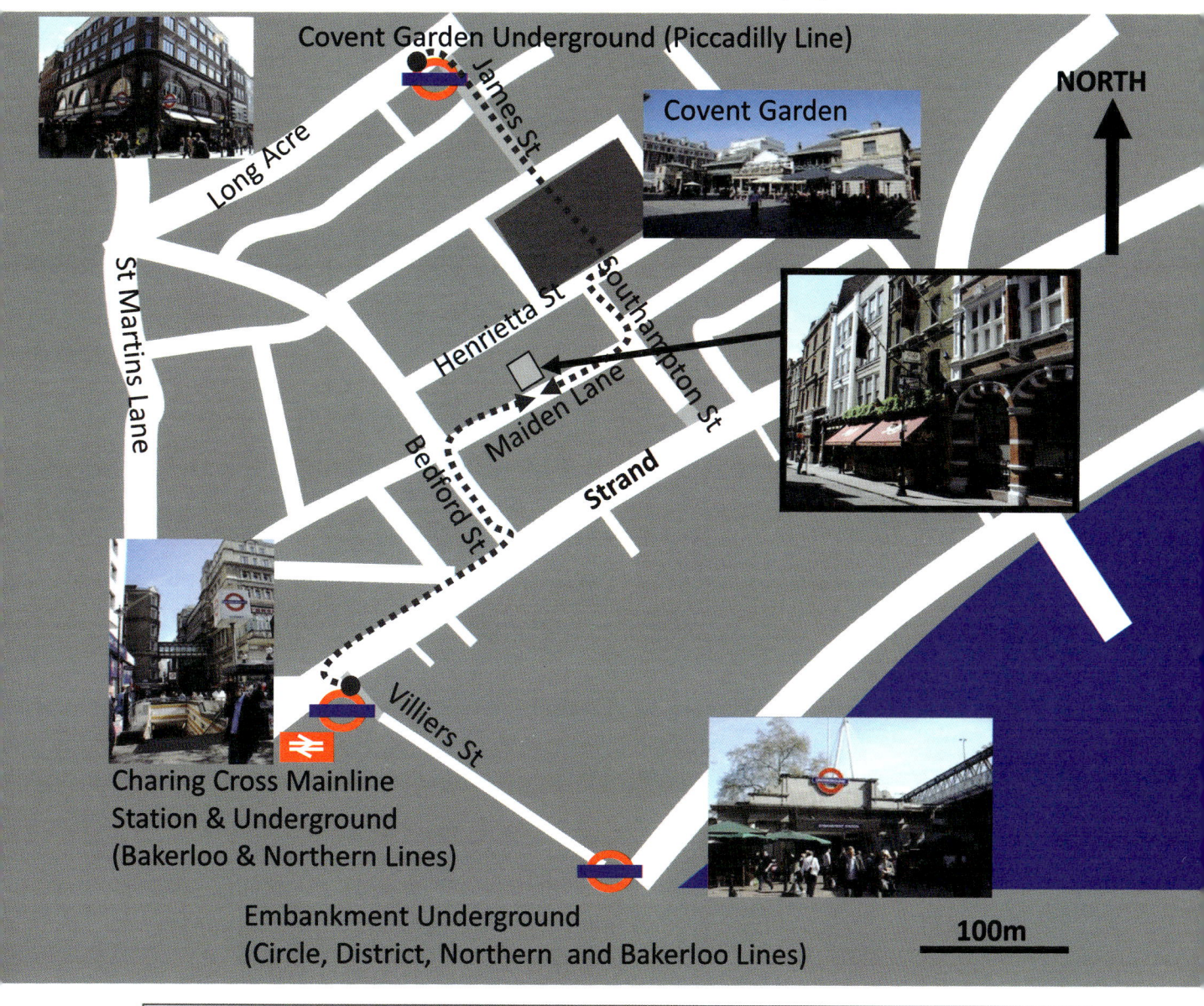

Covent Garden Underground (Piccadilly Line)

Covent Garden

NORTH

Long Acre

James St

St Martins Lane

Henrietta St

Southampton St

Bedford St

Maiden Lane

Strand

Villiers St

Charing Cross Mainline Station & Underground (Bakerloo & Northern Lines)

Embankment Underground (Circle, District, Northern and Bakerloo Lines)

100m

Open seven days a week (need to book):	
Monday to Saturday:	12.00-23.45
Sundays:	12.00-22.45
www.rules.co.uk	

Game and Puddings
Background

This recommendation encompasses two distinct foods Game and Puddings. Game is a fairly self explanatory concept found widely throughout Europe but puddings are a particularly British tradition.

Game is meat from animals hunted for food, and in Britain game generally is used to refer to game birds (such as pheasant and grouse), wildfowl (such as ducks or geese), rabbits and deer. The meat is usually served either roasted or pan fried with a sauce, in pies or stews.

The word "Pudding" as used here refers to desserts, usually fairly heavy and served with custard. Typically traditional puddings are formed by mixing various ingredients with butter, flour, eggs, suet. These puddings are baked, steamed or boiled.

Puddings have a very important place in English culture, due to school dinners. School meals were first introduced to state schools in the 1870s to combat the high levels of malnutrition amongst children in poor areas. In 1944 it was made compulsory to provide school dinners, though since the 1980's they are no longer free for all. This has resulted in traditional "school dinner" meals becoming part of many people's childhood. "School puddings" in particular are often fondly remembered and the phrase refers to hot desserts served in school, such as spotted dick, jam roly poly and treacle sponge pudding all served with custard.

Golden Treacle Sponge Pudding
with Custard
Rules

Game and Puddings at Rules Recommended Menu

Rules' menu is full of traditional in-season foods. The dishes vary with the game season so it is difficult to recommend specific meal that would be available through out the year. If one particularly wants to experience wildfowl or game birds then it is important to go in the second half of the year after August.

Note the traditional puddings, particularly Golden Treacle Sponge Pudding with Custard and Sticky Toffee & Date Pudding with Butterscotch sauce are quite filling but are a must to try. Particularly the first is served in almost all schools therefore brings back real memories of school days. Rules' version is perfect.

It is recommended to take three leisurely courses. Particularly nice is a late lunch around 2 o'clock when the restaurant gets quieter.

For your starter try Morecambe Bay Potted Shrimps with Watercress Salad and Melba Toast. Or alternatively try Rabbit with Stornoway Black Pudding, Quail's Egg and Cox's Apple (if it is on the menu).

It is recommended to follow this by Venison Loin (dependent on time of year) with Pear, Roast Chicory & Spiced Ruby Plums. Served with creamed mash.

For dessert try Golden Treacle Sponge Pudding with custard which is a traditional pudding.

Prices*: starters range from £7.50 to £15.00; main courses are around £25 per person; and puddings £7.50.

*2010 prices.

Venison Loin
with Pear, Roast Chicory & Spiced Ruby Plums and Creamed Mash
Rules

English Breakfast
Simpson's-in-the-Strand

Simpson's-in-the Strand
Background and Recommended Meal

Simpson's-in-the-Strand opened in 1828 as a chess club and coffee house called The Grand Cigar Divan. In 1848 it became "Simpson's Grand Divan Tavern" and focused on food, becoming known for its carving of roasts at the table, a practice that continues today. After a refurbishment in 1904 it changed its name to the present day Simpson's-in-the-Strand.

Housed in the Savoy Buildings, for much of its history Simpson's-in-the-Strand has been part of the Savoy Group, though it is now independently managed.

It focuses on traditional English food with a strong emphasis on seasonal food and is famed for it clubby atmosphere and roast meats carved at the table, you can even book carving lessons. It is recommended for game, roasts (particularly at lunchtime) and for cooked breakfast. The roasts are presented from antique domed silver trolleys and carved at the table as has been done for the last 150 years. It makes a great alternative venue for mid week roast lunch.

Simpson's has served breakfasts since 1994 and it provides an almost perfect traditional English breakfast experience. Note the breakfasts are large. It is an excellent place for a business breakfast, especially if you book a booth.

The recommended meal is The Ten Deadly Sins, which consists of:- Cumberland sausage, streaky and back bacon, Stornoway black pudding, fried mushrooms, baked tomato, egg (fried, poached or scrambled), lamb kidney, fried bread, bubble & squeak and baked beans. Included in the price is toast, pastries, freshly brewed coffee & tea, choice of cereals, porridge or half a grapefruit, orange juice, apple juice or grapefruit juice. The recommended breakfast costs £21* per person excluding service.

*2010 prices

Simpson's-in-the-Strand
Strand

Simpson's-in-the-Strand
Strand

Simpson's-in-the-Strand
100 Strand, WC2R 0EW
Tel +44(0)20 7836 9112

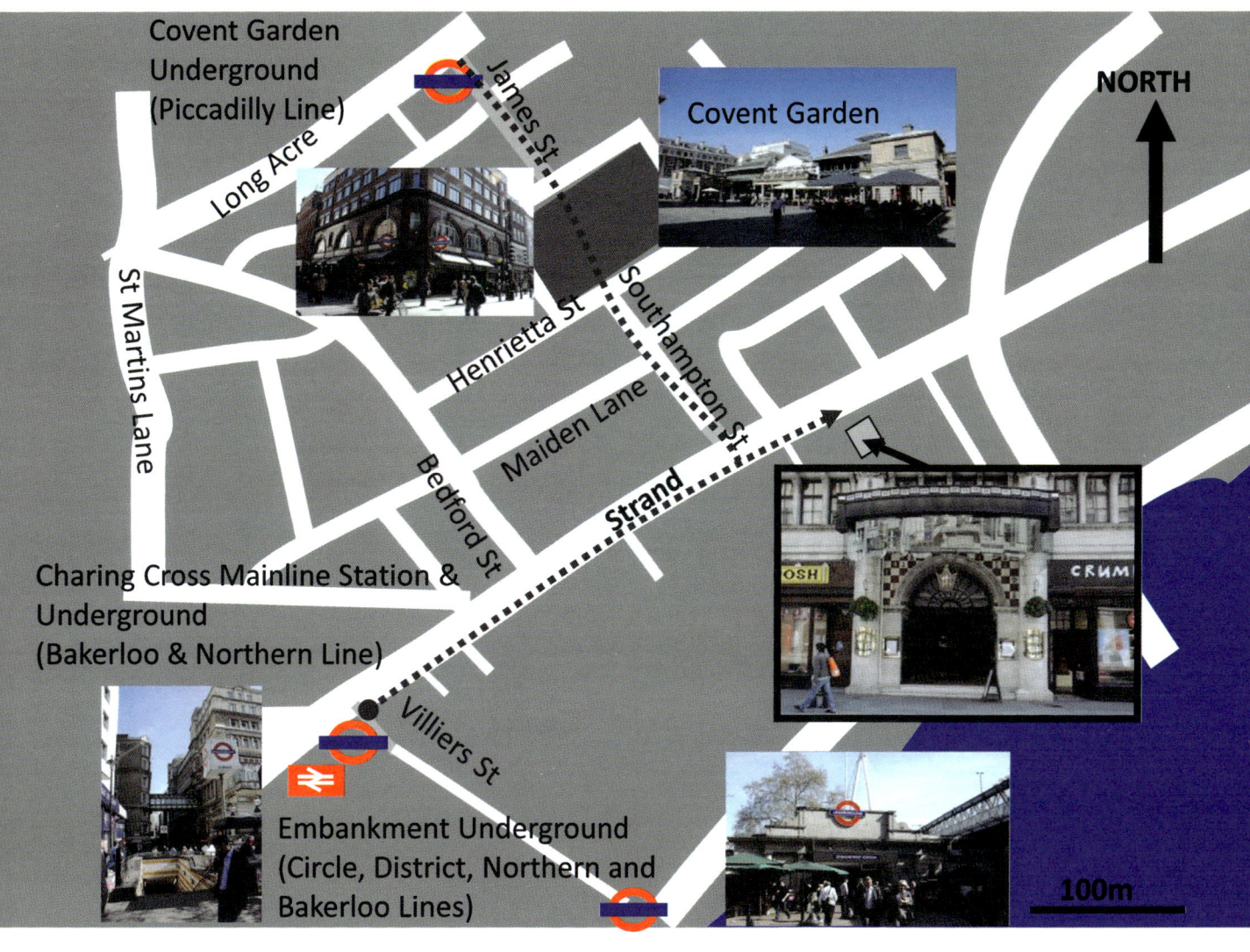

Covent Garden Underground (Piccadilly Line)

Covent Garden

NORTH

Long Acre

James St

Henrietta St

Southampton St

St Martins Lane

Maiden Lane

Bedford St

Strand

Charing Cross Mainline Station & Underground (Bakerloo & Northern Line)

Villiers St

Embankment Underground (Circle, District, Northern and Bakerloo Lines)

100m

Open 7 days a week		
Breakfast:	Monday to Friday:	07.15-10.30
Lunch:	Monday to Saturday:	12.15-14.45
	Sunday:	12.15-15.00
Dinner:	Monday to Saturday:	17.45-22.45
	Sunday:	18.00-21.00
www.simpsonsinthestrand.co.uk		

English Breakfast Background

The Oxford English Dictionary defines an English Breakfast as a substantial breakfast including hot cooked food such as bacon and eggs. English Breakfast is traditionally a fried meal eaten at breakfast, though it is often served now for brunch or even lunch. Whilst the origins are not clear it is often associated with farmer's breakfasts / the countryside and in different guises is found throughout the British Isles.

Now-a-days it is viewed as a treat to be eaten at weekends or when staying in a hotel. All hotels in the UK will offer a cooked or English Breakfast, though often as a buffet rather than cooked to order. The best cook to order, source local ingredients, free range eggs and offer specialty British sausages and black pudding. Black pudding and sausages in particular can vary greatly in standard and good ones will make a cooked breakfast. Regional variations such as Scottish Breakfast, Irish Breakfast and Ulster Fry up also exist.

The standard ingredients of a traditional cooked or full English breakfast are: bacon, sausages, fried eggs (but you will be offered poached or scrambled), fried or grilled tomatoes, fried mushrooms and fried bread usually served with a cup of tea. Black pudding is added in some regions. Also sometimes you will be offered bubble and squeak which is shallow-fried leftover vegetables with potato.

Note there are other cooked breakfasts that are traditional such as Kippers (fried or grilled smoked herring), Kedgeree (flaked smoked haddock, rice, boiled eggs, curry powder and cream) and Devilled Kidneys (lamb kidneys cooked in a spicy sauce).

If not eating in your Hotel, Simpsons-in-the-Strand is an excellent experience. For a more continental experience try The Wolseley on Piccadilly.

The Ten Deadly Sins
Simpson's-in-the-Strand

Afternoon Tea
Fortnum & Mason

Fortnum & Mason Background

Fortnum & Mason has been an institution on Piccadilly since 1707 and has held Royal warrants since 1863. Set up as a grocer by Hugh Mason and William Fortnum, by 1744 it began its long history as a purveyor of teas. It pioneered the development of ready made luxury food and since Victorian times has been renowned for luxury picnic hampers. Now a department store, Fortnum & Mason is still more famous for its tea and food; its teas and biscuits make a perfect gift.

Afternoon tea can be taken in any of Fortnum and Mason's restaurants, but St James's Restaurant on the Fourth Floor is the recommended location for the most elegant afternoon tea. Its classic Afternoon Tea is served with a choice of tea, with over 70 different blends and single estate teas to choose from, and is accompanied by a traditional menu of finger sandwiches, miniature cakes and scones, plus a plate of canapés. The cake selection varies and you have a choice of cakes. Note extra refills of all dishes are offered.

Whilst afternoon tea is served all afternoon, the restaurant is busiest after 4pm and is often wonderfully quiet from 2pm. Afternoon tea is served in the soft seating area on coffee tables.

Fortnum & Mason
Piccadilly

St James Restaurant (4th Floor)
Fortnum & Mason
Piccadilly

St James Restaurant (4th Floor)
Fortnum & Mason
181 Piccadilly, W1A 1ER
Reservations Tel: +44(0)845 602 5694

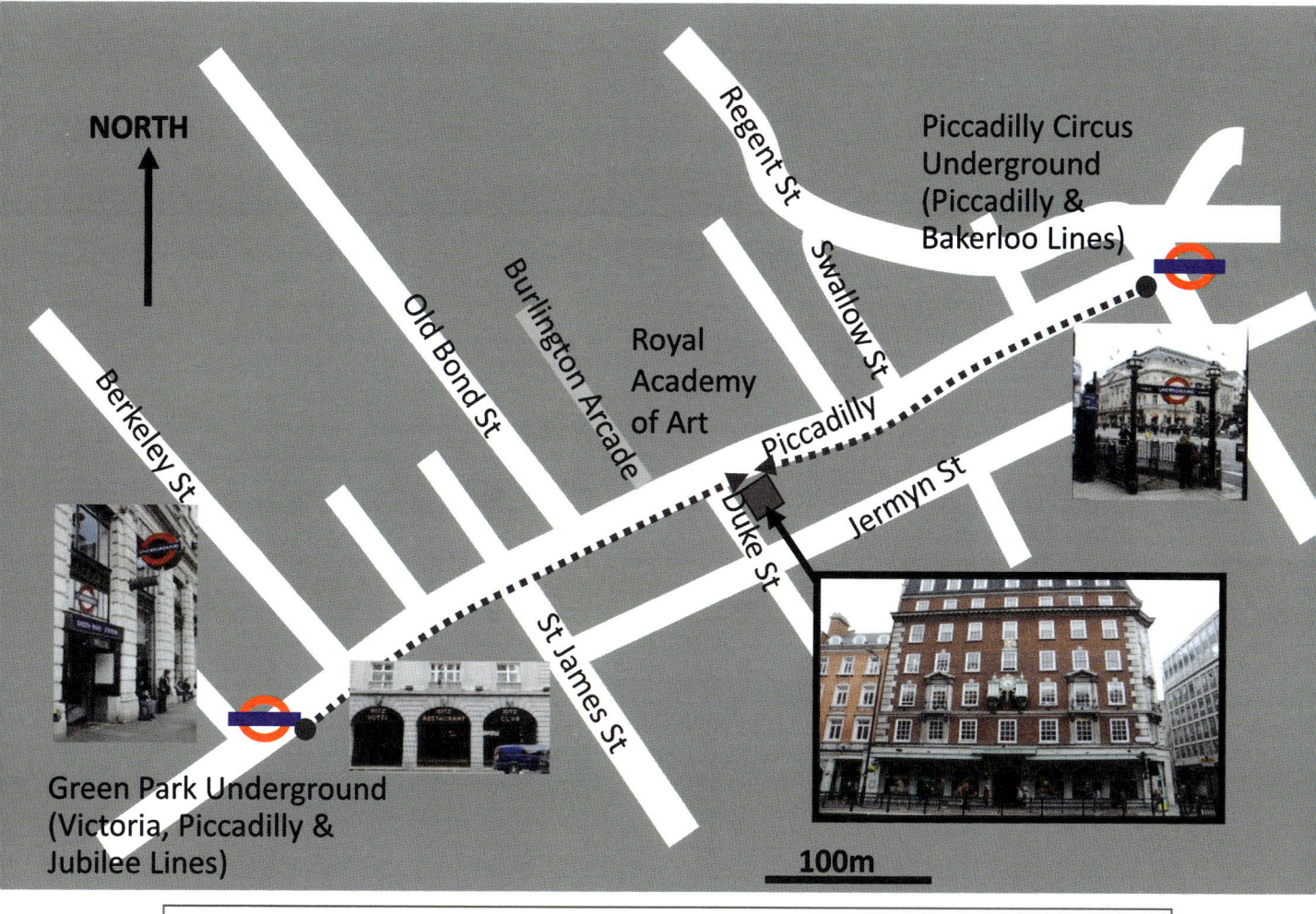

Open seven days a week: Reservations recommended

Monday – Saturday	Lunch	12.00-14:00
	Afternoon Tea	12.00-18:30
Sunday	Lunch	12.00-14:30
	Afternoon Tea	12.00-16:30

Dress Code: Elegant, for gentlemen no shorts or open toe sandals, ideally jacket and tie.

www.fortnumandmason.com

Afternoon Tea Background

Afternoon Tea has its origins in the 17th Century; when Catherine of Braganza, wife of Charles II, brought the practice of drinking tea in the afternoon with her from Portugal. The form that we now call Afternoon Tea, essentially a light meal eaten between 15.00 and 17.00, dates from the early 19th century. Anna Maria Russell, Duchess of Bedford, is believed to be the person who transformed afternoon tea in England into a late-afternoon meal rather than a simple refreshment. While living in Woburn Abbey she started taking tea with a snack in the afternoon in her boudoir. She continued the practice on her return to London inviting friends to join her and soon other fashionable hostesses copied the idea and Afternoon Tea became part of British Society.

Traditionally, Afternoon Tea comprises of loose tea brewed in a teapot and served in teacups with milk; sandwiches (customarily cucumber, egg and cress, ham and smoked salmon); scones with clotted cream and strawberry jam (the clotted cream can be replaced by butter); and cakes and pastries. The food is served on a tiered stand.

A formal Afternoon Tea is, nowadays, usually taken as a treat in a hotel or tea shop. In London Piccadilly is synonymous with elegant Afternoon teas from The Ritz to Fortnum & Mason and more recently The Wolseley. Fortnum & Mason has been chosen for two reasons, excellent afternoon tea in a historic location and ease of getting a booking. Note The Ritz can take three to five months to get a booking.

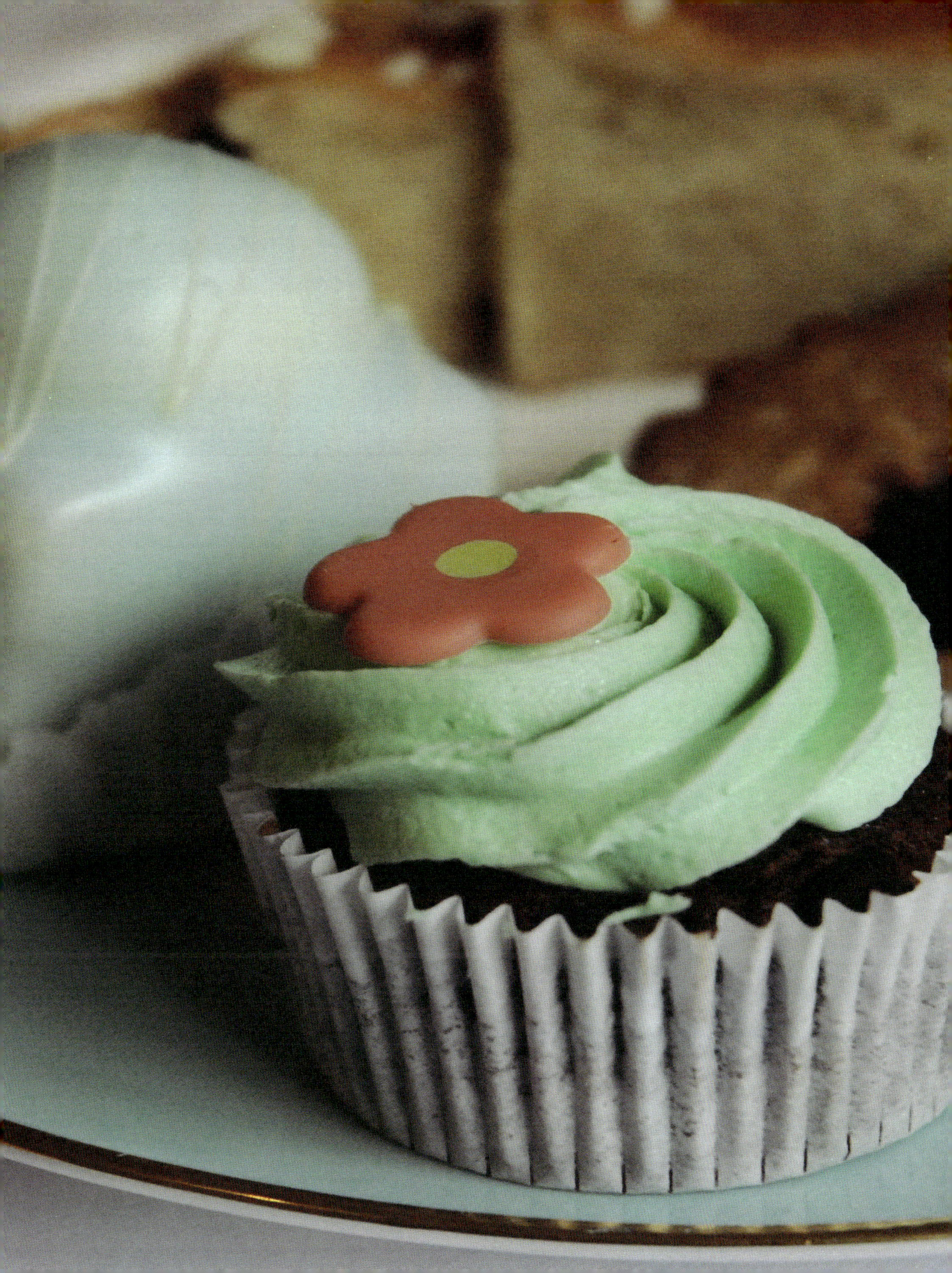

Afternoon Tea at Fortnum & Mason Recommended Menu

Afternoon Tea is as much an experience as a meal. Afternoon Tea at the St James Restaurant is served in a formal soft seating area with settees and coffee tables. The recommended meal is a set meal "Fortnum's Classic Afternoon". Below are the items included, please note that refills for the tea and also additional scones, cakes and sandwiches are available on request within the standard price. The price* is £32 person plus £4 service. The selection of tea to choose from is huge and very high quality, in terms of Afternoon Tea it is recommended to take the Royal Blend. Note the tea is loose leaved so ensure you use the strainer to ensure no leaves in your tea.

Fortnum's Classic Afternoon Tea is served on a tiered cake stand and consists of:- selection of canapés; finger sandwiches and rolls; plain and fruit scones with Somerset clotted cream and jam preserve (recommend strawberry preserve); lemon drizzle cake, raspberry jam biscuits, madeleine's and a choice of cakes from the tray.

* 2010 prices

Afternoon Tea
Fortnum & Mason

The Gastropub
The Anchor & Hope

The Anchor & Hope
Background

The Anchor & Hope is a casual gastropub south of the River Thames close to Waterloo Station and the increasingly popular and busy South Bank. It opened in 2003 and since then is regularly ranked and reviewed as one of the best gastropubs in London.

Located close to the Old Vic on very much a local street and off the tourist beaten track, the Anchor & Hope is not much from the outside. However inside it has a busy informal atmosphere, drinks are served in tumblers for example. There is a strict no booking policy (except on Sunday when you need to book), and you have to turn up and wait for a table. It is recommended that you get there early and are prepared to hang around having a drink (note you need to put your name down for a table so ask one of the staff). Weekday lunch is much quieter generally and you should have no problem to get a table, especially around 12.00.

The Anchor & Hope has a strong seasonal influenced menu that changes twice daily. This makes recommending a specific list of dishes somewhat problematic; however the meat sharing dishes, when on the menu, will blow your socks off and well worth trying.

Insider's tip: come either by foot or by taxi and cross the River Thames via Waterloo Bridge to see one of the grandest views of London, the sweeping views of the Thames looking towards St Paul's Cathedral.

The Anchor & Hope
Southwark

The Anchor & Hope
Southwark

The Anchor & Hope
36 The Cut, Southwark SE1 8LP
Tel: +44(0)20 7928 9898

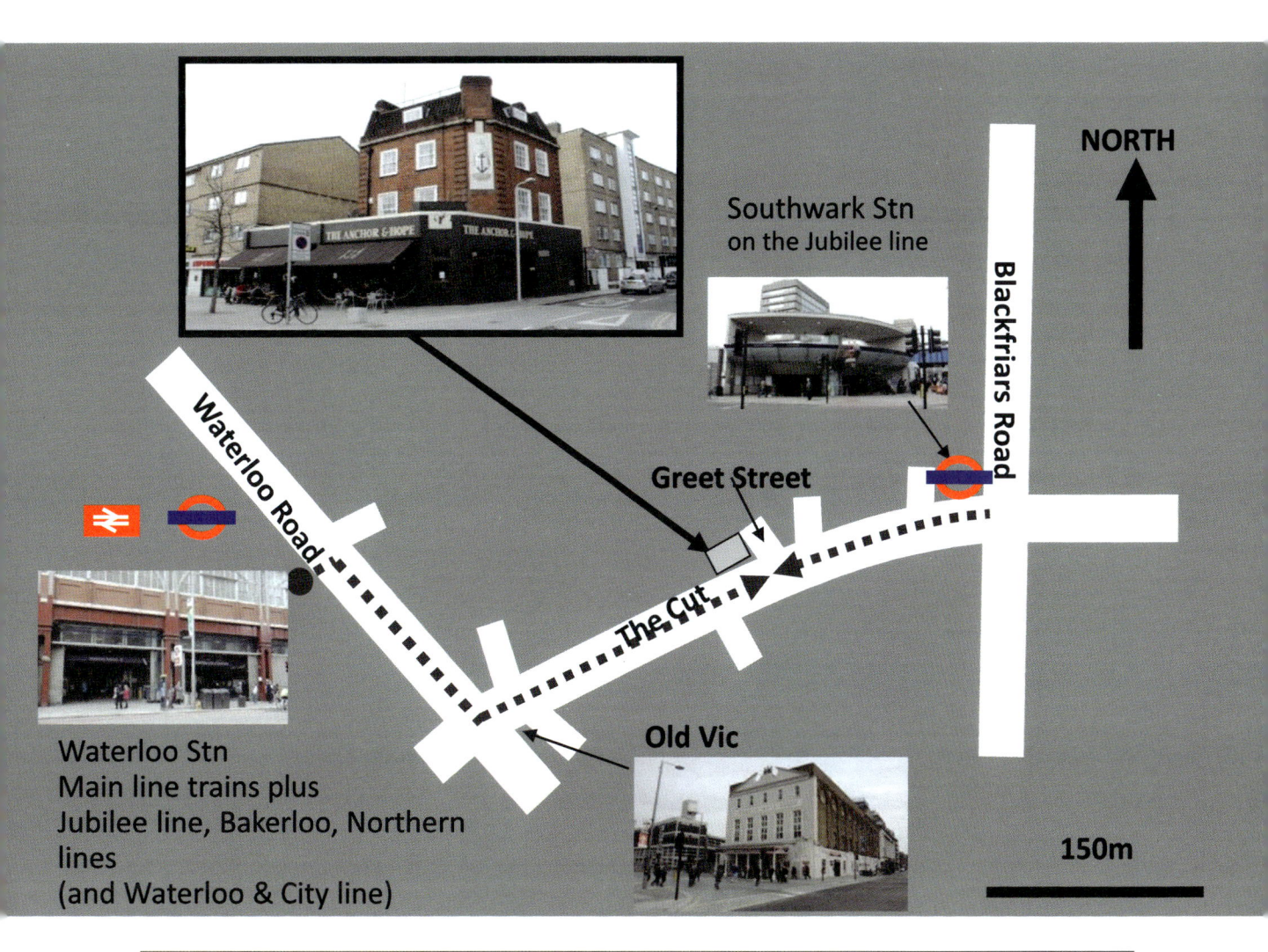

Southwark Stn on the Jubilee line

Greet Street

Waterloo Road

Blackfriars Road

The Cut

NORTH

Waterloo Stn
Main line trains plus
Jubilee line, Bakerloo, Northern lines
(and Waterloo & City line)

Old Vic

150m

Open seven days a week (Note there is a NO BOOKING policy):
Monday:	17.00-23.00
Tuesday-Saturday:	11.00-23.00
Sunday:	12.30-17.00 (one lunch sitting at 14.00)

The Gastropub
Background and Recommended Menu

The term gastropub, a combination of the words gastronomy and pub, was first used in the early 1990s to describe a new breed of pubs whose focus was on quality food. The first gastropub was opened when David Eyre and Mike Belben took over The Eagle pub in Clerkenwell, London.

The concept of gastropubs has now spread across the country and has established a strong new genre of food establishments. Most focus on British foods with strong seasonal connections and often local sourced meats and foods.

Most gastropubs have been set up in renovated local pubs, whilst more informal than restaurants they tend to be more formal than the usual local pub. Generally they are visited for food not for just for a drink and are often sought out by foodies when they visit a new area.

At The Anchor and Hope the menu is strongly seasonal and changes twice a day, and it is therefore not possible to recommend a specific menu.

Crab
The Anchor & Hope

Poached Leg of Duck and Lentils
The Anchor & Hope

New Potatoes
The Anchor & Hope

Curry
Punjab

Punjab Restaurant Background

The Punjab restaurant was established in 1951 at the top of Neal Street in Covent Garden, within walking distance of the Indian High Commission. The restaurant can trace it roots to an earlier restaurant set up in 1947 by Gurbachan Maan in Aldgate, East London, hence the 1947 in the logo; it has been run by the same family since and claims to be the oldest North Indian restaurant in London.

The restaurant is housed in a 300 year old listed building and spreads into the two adjacent properties. Its layout is higgledy-piggledy but the décor and furnishing are typical of traditional Indian restaurants in Britain. The black and white pictures lend a nice finishing touch to the ambience.

The Punjab is known as a safe place to get a good curry in central London, it serves the standard dishes one would expect and due to its high turnover, the spices are always fresh and the food well prepared and balanced. It is regularly voted one of the top 100 Indian Restaurants in the UK by the UK Curry Club.

The Punjab's clientele are a mixture of local Londoners working in the area and tourists, plus later at night it is very busy with people coming out of the pubs. At lunch time the restaurant is relatively quiet and there is no need to book. On an evening it is recommended to book unless you are prepared to wait.

Punjab
Neal Street, Covent Garden

Punjab
Neal Street, Covent Garden

Punjab,
80 Neal St, Covent Garden, WC2H 9PA
Tel +44 (0)20 7836 9787

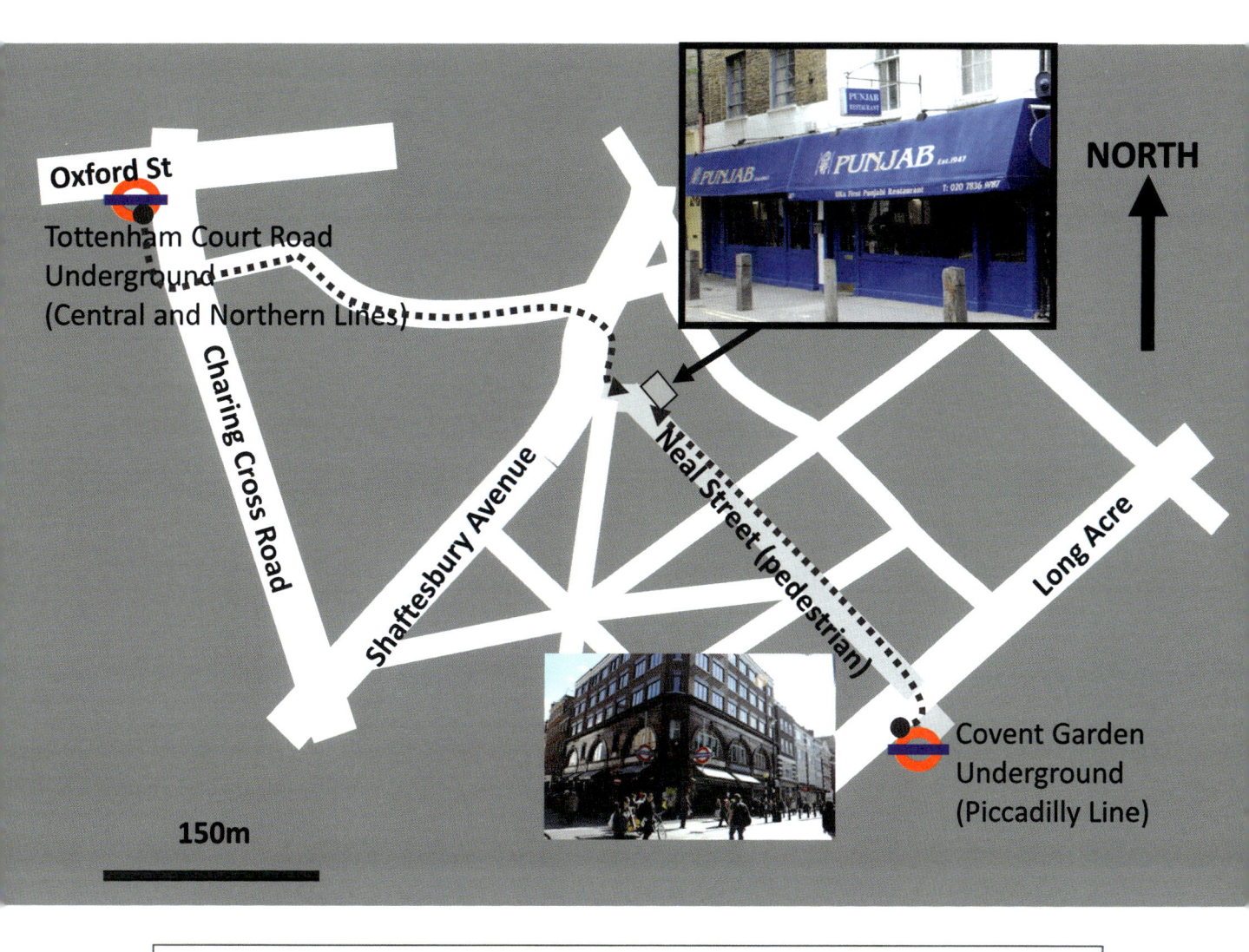

Open seven days a week:

Monday– Saturday:	Lunch	12.00-15.00
	Dinner	18.00-23.30
Sunday:	Lunch	12.00-15.00
	Dinner	18.00-22.30

www.punjab.co.uk

Curry – Chicken Tikka Masala Background

Whilst purists will say that Curry is not English or even British food, Britain's history with Curry goes back to the 17th Century, and it is by some counts the most popular food to go out and eat in Britain.

The dish chosen, Chicken Tikka Masala, is the most popular dish in Indian Restaurants and in 2007 a survey found it was the most popular dish in Britain. Going for a curry or "Indian" after the pub has become almost the cultural norm for a great proportion of the population in the UK.

There are claims that Chicken Tikka Masala was actually invented in the UK, possibly in Glasgow, though there is some evidence that it was based on Mughal dish. However, no matter what are its origins it is without a doubt a dish very strongly associated with Britain and served here more widely than in any other country.

The dish is made of chicken cooked or roasted in a tandoor and then cooked in a creamy tomato sauce. The sauce is very lightly spiced and is generally a bright orange / bright red colour. It is now sold in all traditional Indian restaurants in Britain.

The restaurant chosen, the Punjab, is one of the oldest in central London and serves North Indian food. London also has two areas further out that are famous for Indian food, just east of The City there is Brick Lane and in the west fairly close to Heathrow is Southall a predominantly Indian area.

Chicken Tikka Masala
with Naan and Kali Dall
Punjab

Curry at the Punjab Recommended Meal

The Punjab's menu is clear and easy to use for those uninitiated in the delights of Indian food. The Punjab's menu includes all the traditional dishes one would expect to find in an Indian restaurant in Britain. The recommended meal includes the most "English" of curries, Chicken Tikka Masala which is mildly spiced. If one wants a more spicy recommendation it is recommended that you substitute Chicken Tikka Masala with Chicken Madras, a very standard hot spiced curry.

The recommended meal is two courses with a pre-starter. Start with two plain Papadums with chutney and pickles, followed by a starter of Kadu Puri (pumpkin on crispy Indian bread). For the main course have Chicken Tikka Masala (the recipe dates from 1973), with plain boiled rice and a Butter Naan. Naan is unleavened flat bread cooked in a Tandoor oven and should be eaten hot and dipped by hand in the Tikka Masala sauce or Dall. If hungry order a side dish of Kali Dall (Black lentils). To drink, either still water or Indian Kingfisher Beer.

The recommended meal costs approximately £26 including service.

Kadu Puri
Pumpkin on a crispy Indian bread
Punjab

Jellied Eels & Pie 'n' Mash
M.Manze

M.Manze
Background

Well off the beaten path, Manze is located south of Tower Bridge in a very traditional working class area of London called Bermondsey.

M.Manze is the oldest traditional Pie 'n' Mash and Eel shop in London. Originally established in 1891 by Robert Cooke; Michele Manze, his son-in-law, bought it in 1902. Today M.Manze is still a family business, run by his three grandsons. They serve traditional Pie 'n' Mash and Eels (jellied or stewed) using the same 1902 recipe, in an atmospheric traditional tiled shop.

The Manzes were originally from Italy and immigrated to London in 1878 (when Michele was three), setting up an ice cream business in Bermondsey at number 85 Tower Bridge Road, next door to the current M.Manze shop. Spotting the opportunity for cheap substantial food Michele took over the Pie 'n' Mash shop next door.

By 1927 M.Manze had five outlets. At the height of its popularity the Manzes (including his brothers) had fifteen Pie "n" Mash shops. Many of these are now closed (with two destroyed during the Second World War) but M.Manze still has three Pie 'n' Mash shops.

Note: M.Manze is very casual local café and is not definitely not suitable for business lunches.

M.Manze
Tower Bridge Rd. Bermondsey

M.Manze
Tower Bridge Rd, Bermondsey

M.Manze
87 Tower Bridge Rd, SE1 4TW
Tel: +44 (0)20 7407 2985

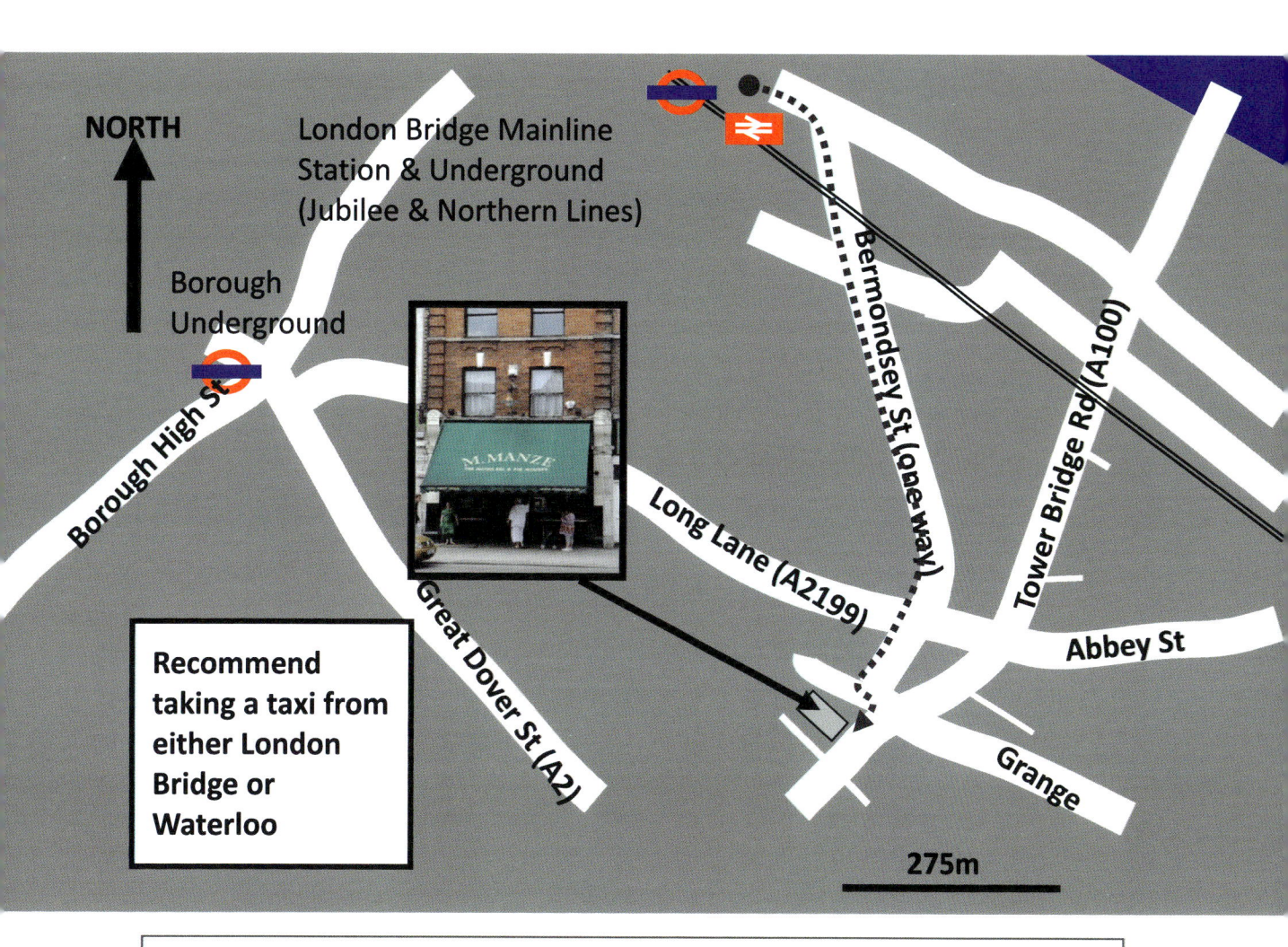

Recommend taking a taxi from either London Bridge or Waterloo

Open for **LUNCH ONLY** 6 days a week:

Monday:	11.00-14.00
Tuesday-Thursday:	10.30-14.00
Friday:	10.00-14.30
Saturday:	10.00-14.45

www.manze.co.uk

Jellied Eels and Pie 'n' Mash Background

As said before fish have played a major role in London's food history. Of all the food traditions eels are the most uniquely associated with London. Pie 'n' Mash and Eels are intrinsically connected with being Cockney (i.e. born in the East End of London). Eel Pie and Mash houses or shops have been around at least since early 18th century. They specialise in eels particularly jellied and also beef pies with mash.

Jellied Eels are the most famous London dish, though not widely eaten now, in the late 19th century and early 20th century these were common dishes in the East of London.

The eels are typically caught locally in the River Thames or Estuary. The dish is made from boiling chopped eels with herbs and then allowing an eel jelly to form when cooling. The taste is reputedly similar to that of pickled herring, but the texture means that this is certainly an acquired taste.

As said earlier, pies are a stable part of English cooking. In London this comes in the form of specialised Pie 'n' Mash Shops, selling cheap pies and mash plus jellied eels. Traditionally, the pies were made from scraps of beef and vegetables under a pastry crust. The pie and mashed potatoes are covered in parsley gravy or "liquor"- most Pie 'n' Mash shops have their own secret recipe.

This type of food is cheap, plentiful working class food. Price* of jellied eels at M.Manze is £3.05 and for two meat pies with mash £4.50.

*2010 prices

Jellied Eels
M.Manze

Two Pies 'n' Mash with Liquor
Manze

M.Manze
Tower Bridge Road Bermondsey

Fish & Chips Golden Hind

Golden Hind
Background and Recommended Meal

Central London is relatively devoid of traditional Fish and Chip shops as found in most suburbs, however the Golden Hind is a wonderful example of the London Fish and Chip café. Located at the top of Marylebone Lane the Golden Hind is located an easy walk from Oxford Street along an interesting quiet lane.

Set up in 1914, the Golden Hind is a long established favourite with locals and students alike. Only owned by five owners in its long history, their names are recorded on a blackboard on the wall of the restaurant. The current owner Mr Christou is Greek and has owned it since 2002.

The décor of the café is very traditional with dark wood-stained furniture, black-and-white photographs depicting the local area and an original decommissioned art deco fryer by F Ford of Halifax at the rear of the seating area.

The menu is short and simple: cod, haddock, fishcakes, rock salmon, plaice, skate, whole tail scampi and halibut – all available either fried (in batter) or steamed; chips; peas or salad. Price for a small cod is £4.90 plus £1.70 for chips*. Food can be eaten in or taken away. Note there is no license for alcohol, but you can bring your own.

It is relatively quiet at lunch time and is a nice place to eat even by oneself, though it gets busy in the evening. Note this is a casual café, and whilst during the day is mainly frequented by local workers it is not suitable for business entertaining.

The recommended meal is small cod and chips with a side order of mushy peas and accompanied by a traditional cup of tea.

*2010 prices

Golden Hind
Marylebone

Golden Hind
73 Marylebone Lane, W1U 2PN
Tel: +44 (0)20 7486 3644

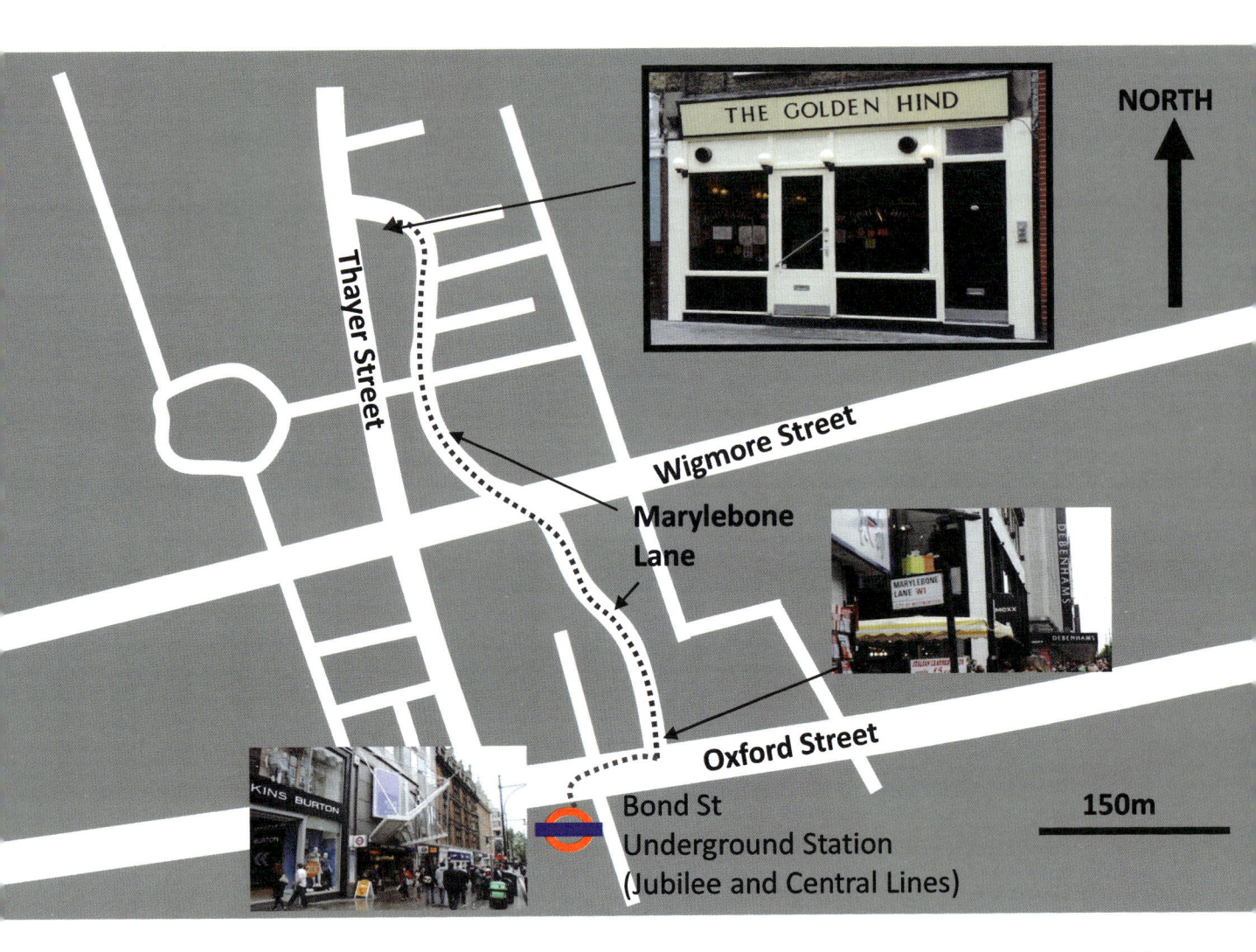

Open six days a week:		
Monday-Friday	Lunch	12.00-15.00
Monday-Saturday	Dinner	18.00-22.00

Fish & Chips
Background

Fish and Chips are the best known British dish, and date back to the 19th Century. It is believed that the combination of fish with chips first happened in 1860 and was pioneered by Joseph Malin who opened the first Fish and Chip shop in London who combined "fish fried in the Jewish fashion" with chips.

The development of large industrial cities (particularly in the north of England and Scotland) during the later stages of the 19th Century spurred on the expansion of the Fish and Chip trade. This expansion was driven by the development of the stream trawler combined with the wide spread rail network – this allowed fish landed one day to be on sale in inland cities by the next day. Fish and Chips became the food of the working masses, with most neighbourhoods having a Fish and Chip shop.

From the start Fish and Chips were positioned as cheap nourishing food, a positioning that remains even today with approximately 9,000 Fish and Chip shops selling roughly a quarter of all white fish sold in the UK.

Fish and Chips are traditionally sold as a take away meal wrapped in paper (originally newspaper) and served with salt and vinegar (malt vinegar). The menu tends to be limited, selling chips (fried chipped potatoes) with battered white fish, most commonly cod. Other fish are typically offered: haddock, plaice or pollock, plus in the South of England, skate, hake and dogfish. Nowadays, it is common for deep fried sausages (both battered and plain), pies, fish cakes, and chicken to be offered in addition. In terms of vegetables the only one usually offered is mushy peas.

Chips are thick cut potato batons deep fried originally in lard but nowadays more often in vegetable oil. The best are part fried and then refried creating a crisp outside with a very soft inside. The battered fish is deep fried in a simple water and flour batter (often with baking soda or little vinegar to create lightness).

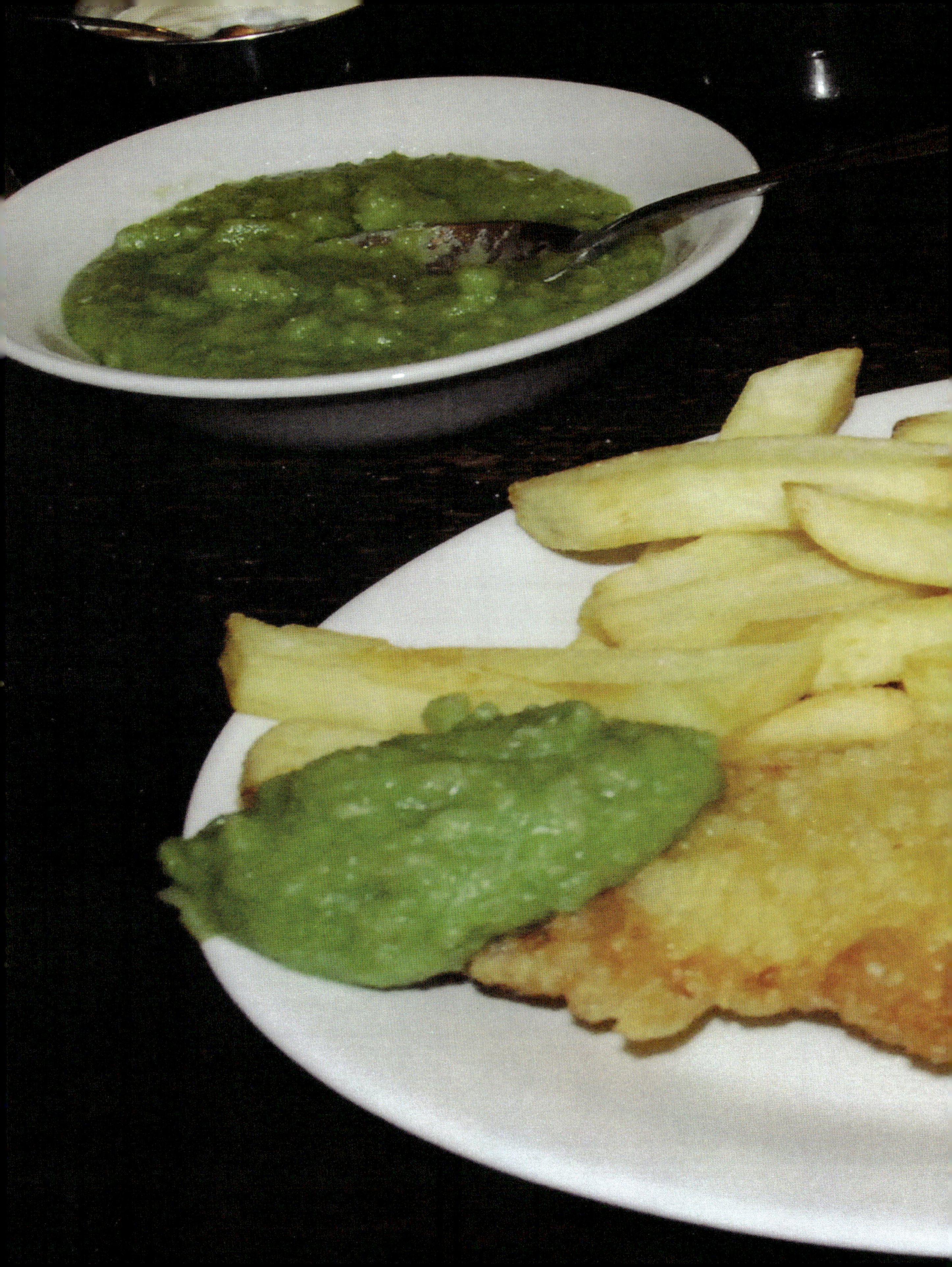

Fish & Chips with Mushy Peas
Golden Hind

The Epilogue

Epilogue

London has a long food history going back to Roman times, generally focused on robust meat or fish dishes often humble in origin. Viewed from afar the culinary quality of the food in London has often been questioned. The traditional restaurants and foods chosen in this guide are great representations of traditional English food and allow the visitor to experience wonderful food of good quality. If one is interested in finding more about London and its food history try chapters 34 and 35 of Peter Ackroyd's "London the Biography".

This guide has focused on traditional restaurants and foods, it has not covered the new wave of contemporary British restaurants. In the last fifteen to twenty years the restaurant scene in London has changed immeasurably. From being a gastronomic back water with a reputation of poor food. The London restaurant scene has become vibrant and high quality. Even more surprising has been the revitalization of traditional dishes made using local British seasonal ingredients.

If you want to experience high quality contemporary British food then in addition to Roast (already covered in the guide) I would recommend the two following restaurants as worth a visit. Both are located towards the City.

- St. John (Farringdon close to Smithfield Market), 26 St John Street, EC1M 4AY. Tel +44 (0)207251 0848.

- Canteen (Spitalfields), Address 2 Crispin Place, Spitalfields, E1 6DW. Tel +44 (0)845 686 1122.

St. John is one of the pioneers of the contemporary British food movement. Located in an old converted 19th Century smokehouse, now painted white with a functional but elegant atmosphere, you enter via a covered alley.

Heavily focused on meat and using all parts of the animal, the menu mixes innovative new dishes with old favourites.

Canteen is a different type of restaurant with all-day menus served at large shared tables. It focuses on very British dishes served well in an informal atmosphere.

Finally the other typical recommendation asked for by visitors is for a good traditional pub. The Salisbury in St Martin's Lane (on the edge of Covent Garden) was established in 1892 and is a very traditional London pub with beautiful etched glass and a magnificent interior. Alternatively you can try the Guinea Grill in Mayfair, which is small, intimate and serves a good pint.

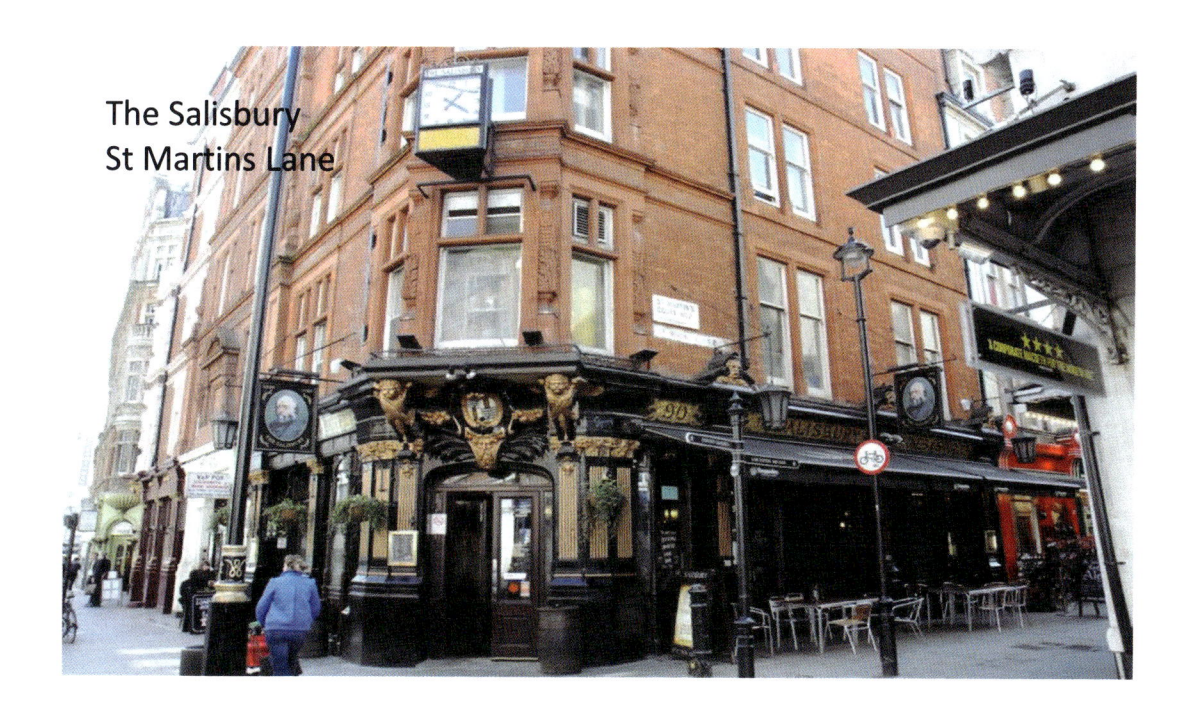

The Salisbury
St Martins Lane

10 places to eat LONDON

About the Author

Tagore Ramoutar has spent over 16 years travelling on business around the world. He would often stay in the same city for over a week or repeatedly visit the same city. He found that after one had been brought out for a couple of business meals, there was always a few spare evenings during which he could either eat in the hotel or explore the local area. This guide is inspired by the joys of exploring the local traditional foods of various cities he has visited.

Made in the USA
Charleston, SC
22 January 2011